D1441085

Sleep-Deprived Nation

Why Sleep Matters

Don Nardo

ReferencePoint Press

San Diego, CA

About the Author

Classical historian, amateur astronomer, and award-winning author Don Nardo has written numerous volumes about scientific topics, including *Destined for Space* (winner of the Eugene M. Emme Award for best astronomical literature); *Tycho Brahe* (winner of the National Science Teaching Association's best book of the year); *Deadliest Dinosaurs*; and *The History of Science*. Nardo, who also composes and arranges orchestral music, lives with his wife, Christine, in Massachusetts.

© 2024 ReferencePoint Press, Inc.
Printed in the United States

For more information, contact:
ReferencePoint Press, Inc.
PO Box 27779
San Diego, CA 92198
www.ReferencePointPress.com

LIBRARY OF CONGRESS CATALOGING-IN-PUBLICATION DATA

Names: Nardo, Don, 1947- author.
Title: Sleep-deprived nation : why sleep matters / by Don Nardo.
Description: San Diego, CA : ReferencePoint Press, Inc., 2024. | Includes bibliographical references.
Identifiers: LCCN 2023001455 (print) | LCCN 2023001456 (ebook) | ISBN 9781678205881 (library binding) | ISBN 9781678205898 (ebook)
Subjects: LCSH: Sleep. | Sleep deprivation. | Teenagers--Sleep. | Sleep disorders in adolescence.
Classification: LCC RA786 .N37 2024 (print) | LCC RA786 (ebook) | DDC 613.7/94--dc23/eng/20230324
LC record available at https://lccn.loc.gov/2023001455
LC ebook record available at https://lccn.loc.gov/2023001456

Contents

The Biggest Chunk of Human Existence

"Blessings light on him that first invented sleep!" wrote Spanish novelist Miguel de Cervantes in 1605 in his immortal *Don Quixote*. "[Sleep] covers a man all over, thoughts and all, like a cloak; it is meat for the hungry, drink for the thirsty, heat for the cold, and cold for the hot. It is the current coin that purchases all the pleasures of the world cheap, and the balance that sets the king and the shepherd, the fool and the wise man [on the same level]."[1]

In describing sleep as a cloak that overshadows seemingly all of life's other activities, Cervantes acknowledged the importance of that daily interval when people temporarily depart the waking world. In fact, no other single activity consumes a bigger chunk of human existence than sleep does.

Many Life Activities Related to Sleep

In 2022 noted sleep expert Gemma Curtis took the time to calculate how that inevitable chunk of people's lives—sleep—compares to other common daily activities. The eye-opening results of her inquiry reveal first that in an ample lifetime of 79 years (or 28,835 days), a person is asleep for the equivalent of some 26 years. That means that for virtually a third of that individual's life, he or she is unconscious and oblivious to the waking world.

The next-largest portion of an average lifetime, Curtis found, is the approximately 13 years devoted to work—that is, making a living. Then comes watching TV (8 years), followed by eating (4.5 years); checking social media and going on vacation (3 years each); going to school (2.5 years, a figure derived by multiplying the

average number of school hours per day times the number of school days in grades 1 through 12); and socializing with family and friends (1 year). The remaining 18 years encompass the thousands of other things a person does in her or his sojourn on the planet.

Curtis also discovered that most of those other non-sleep activities in a person's life are actually related to sleep in various ways. For example, of the 3 years (almost 1,700 days) an average person spends in his or her life checking social media, at least some of it interferes with sleep. Tests show that the light emitted by computers and cell phones can make it harder for a person to get to sleep, even when he or she is tired. About one-third of adults and one-half of young people aged eighteen to twenty-four wake up and check their cell phones at least once in the middle of the night.

Sleep is also related to people's jobs. For instance, if someone gets too few hours of sleep for one or more nights in a row, it can negatively affect the quality of that person's work in the days that follow. Moreover, Curtis explains, getting enough sleep can sometimes determine whether someone even makes it to work at all. "You'll potentially work for the equivalent of 4,821 days during your time here [on earth]," she points out. "Getting there safely can depend on good sleep. It's estimated that 20% of road traffic accidents are sleep-related."[2]

Widespread Sleep Deprivation

These references to a lack of sleep are important because numerous medical studies indicate that large numbers of people in the modern world do not get enough sleep on a fairly regular basis.

About half of young people aged eighteen to twenty-four wake up and check their cell phones at least once in the middle of the night.

In the United States, for example, around a third of Americans do not get the amount of sleep they should. This was the finding of the Centers for Disease Control and Prevention (CDC), which it announced in 2021 after an extensive study of American sleep habits. Furthermore, the CDC reported, overall, 50 million to 70 million Americans "suffer from chronic sleep problems." Disrupted sleep can cause people to fall asleep while driving and can affect long-term health. Lack of sufficient sleep, the CDC goes on, is associated with "chronic diseases, mental illnesses, poor quality of life and well-being [and] some chronic conditions, including obesity and depression."[3]

Hearing this, it is natural to wonder how many hours of sleep a person should ideally get each night. When asked that question, says sleep specialist Dr. Nicola Sunter, most people "put

the figure at around eight hours. While this is a commonly-held belief . . . it's not necessarily correct. Your sleep need is unique to you . . . determined by many factors, including age, genetics, sex, environment, and lifestyle. . . . When it comes to your sleep, there's no one-size-fits-all amount that works for everyone."[4] Considering the fact that so many people do not get as much sleep as they should, Sunter adds, each of us should take the time to find out whether our sleep needs are being met, and if not, we should take any steps necessary to get the amount of sleep we actually require.

Chapter One

What Is Sleep, and Why Is It Important?

Why do people sleep? This question formed the basis of a groundbreaking study reported by a team of University of California, Los Angeles (UCLA) researchers in the prestigious journal *Science Advances* in September 2020. Previous research about sleep conducted by scientists and medical experts over many decades has discovered numerous facts about it. These include how much sleep is optimal for people of various ages and the negative effects on the body of getting too little sleep.

One thing that had always eluded past researchers, however, was determining exactly *why* people sleep. The UCLA team made history by finally solving that riddle. UCLA spokesperson Stuart Wolpert sums up the study's main finding, which is that there are two important reasons for sleep. The UCLA study, he writes, demonstrated

> for the first time that a dramatic change in the purpose of sleep occurs at the age of about 2-and-a-half. Before that age . . . the young brain is busy building and strengthening synapses—the structures that connect [brain cells] to one another. . . . After 2-and-a-half years, however, sleep's primary purpose switches

from brain building to brain maintenance and repair, a role it maintains for the rest of our lives. . . . All animals naturally experience a certain amount of [brain cell] damage during waking hours, and the resulting debris, including damaged genes and proteins within [the cells] can build up. . . . Sleep helps repair this damage and clear the debris—essentially decluttering the brain and taking out the trash.[5]

The Sleep Cycle

Thus, it turns out, the age-old belief that the brain more or less shuts down during sleep is incorrect. The UCLA study conclusively demonstrates that the body's center of intelligence remains amazingly busy during sleep. It uses this time to carry out many diverse and often quite intricate functions that allow it, and of course its owner, to keep functioning normally over time.

To maintain that normal state of being and functioning, sleep experts explain, a person needs to consistently get what has often been described as "a good night's sleep." The problem with that phrase is that the word *good* is far too vague. What exactly is a good night's sleep?

Scientists who study sleep answer that question by describing the four basic stages of sleep. In the first stage, lasting only a few minutes, a person drifts quietly off to of sleep. There follows stage two, in which she or he sleeps lightly for a few more minutes, and stage three, in which the individual's muscles relax and he or she falls into a much deeper sleep for half an hour to an hour.

Then, finally comes the single most crucial sleep stage—REM sleep. Those letters stand for "rapid eye movement." Rachel Y. Moon, who teaches pediatrics

> "Sleep helps repair [brain cell] damage and clear the debris—essentially decluttering the brain and taking out the trash."[5]
>
> —Stuart Wolpert, spokesperson for the University of California, Los Angeles

9

at the George Washington University School of Medicine, explains what happens during REM sleep. She says:

> REM sleep is often referred to as active sleep and is the stage during which most dreams occur. The eyes move rapidly under the closed eyelids, breathing and heart rate become less regular. . . . The first periods of REM sleep of the night usually last for only a few minutes. As the night goes on, however, REM sleep lengthens. This is why many people awaken in the morning while dreaming and may feel as though the entire night has been spent dreaming. Studies in animals and humans suggest that REM sleep is very important. Among other things, it keeps the brain active, allows the brain to form memories, and helps the senses develop.[6]

The sleeper's journey through these four stages is called a sleep cycle. Under normal circumstances, a person will undergo several such cycles in a night. So it is not unusual to move from

Up until the age of about two and a half, the young brain is busy building its connections during sleep. After two and a half years, sleep's primary purpose switches from brain building to brain maintenance and repair.

REM sleep back to stage three and even back to stage two for a while before returning to the REM stage, and so forth. All in all, in an average night the REM periods add up to about 20 to 25 percent of the sleep session, and the person dreams for a total of about two hours or so. Eventually, he or she wakes up and, if the sleep session was long enough, feels physically and mentally refreshed.

How Much Sleep Do We Need?

But what if the sleep session is *not* long enough? In answering that question, sleep experts tend first to establish how much sleep people actually need to feel rested and remain healthy. In that regard, there is no simple answer, because at different stages in their lives, human beings require different amounts of sleep. According to the National Institutes of Health, the vast majority of adults need from seven to nine hours of sleep a night. But younger people ideally require a good deal more sleep to enjoy optimum health.

Sleep scientists have determined that human sleep needs, ranging from youngest to oldest, are as follows:

- Up to the age of three months: fourteen to seventeen hours
- Ages three months to one year: twelve to fifteen hours
- Age two: eleven to fourteen hours
- Ages three to five: ten to thirteen hours
- Ages six to twelve: nine to eleven hours
- Teenagers: eight to ten hours
- Early twenties to age sixty-five: seven to nine hours
- Over sixty-five: seven to eight hours

Contrary to popular opinion, observes Petra Hawker, director of the London Sleep Centre (a medical clinic in England that specializes in sleep disorders), the amount of sleep needed by people

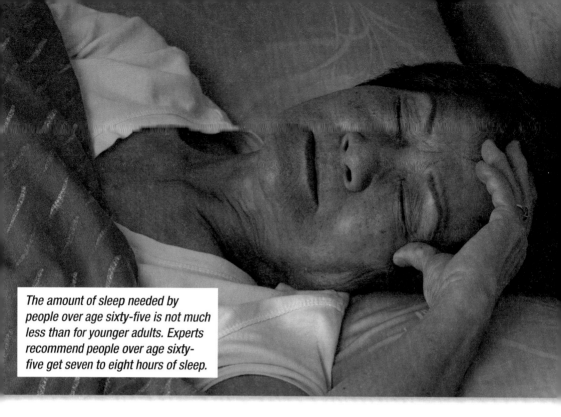

The amount of sleep needed by people over age sixty-five is not much less than for younger adults. Experts recommend people over age sixty-five get seven to eight hours of sleep.

over age sixty-five (seniors) is not much less than for younger adults. Therefore, she writes, "it's a misconception that the need for sleep declines significantly with age. In fact, the amount we need diminishes only a little, but [as seniors] we experience . . . slightly less REM sleep."[7]

Sleep Debt Is Widespread

For many people, getting the recommended number of hours of sleep is difficult. Too little sleep, especially over time, can be harmful to a person's health. When people do not get enough sleep, they become what experts call sleep deficient, or sleep deprived. Sleep scientists also employ the term *sleep debt*, which they apply to individuals who suffer from sleep deprivation. Sleep debt is the total amount of sleep a person loses either in one night or over the course of a longer span of time. It is essentially like a debt one accumulates with

"It's a misconception that the need for sleep declines significantly with age."[7]

—Petra Hawker, director of the London Sleep Centre

money. That is, if an individual takes ten dollars per day out of his or her bank account, at the end of a week the account will be short seventy dollars. If the person suddenly needs that money to pay bills, the seventy dollars will need to be deposited back into the account. In a similar manner, if someone loses two hours of sleep a night for a week, that person will accrue a sleep debt of fourteen hours, and, to be in top health, he or she will have to replace those lost hours sooner or later.

For large numbers of people around the globe, sleep debt is surprisingly and alarmingly widespread, and the United States is no exception. Studies conducted by the National Institutes of Health and the CDC in the early 2000s showed that a great many American adults get fewer than seven hours of sleep a night. This was confirmed by a major study released in 2022 by the Casper Sleep company and the Gallup polling organization. *The State of Sleep in America* study surveyed over three thousand Americans age eighteen and older across the country.

Short Sleepers

"If you paid me a million dollars to sleep eight hours tonight, I couldn't." So says former Utah native Brad Johnson, who turned sixty-five in 2022. He is a so-called short sleeper, a term that describes someone who needs only five or less hours of sleep per night to stay healthy. Johnson comes from a family of short sleepers. They were among the first subjects in studies of short sleeping conducted beginning in 2005 at labs at the University of Utah and later at other US labs. The researchers eventually found three separate genes in the subjects' DNA that cause the strange anomaly. According to *USA Today*'s Elizabeth Weise, these tiny particles exist "in people who are natural short sleepers, needing much less than the normal [seven or eight hours] that most humans require. . . . [The scientists] were able to genetically engineer both fruit flies and mice to have the same [genes] and . . . it appears that humans and mice that carry the mutations get more intense sleep . . . and so need less of it." The scientists also found that short sleepers are a rare breed. Indeed, fewer than 3 percent of Americans carry the genes in question.

Quoted in Sandee LaMotte, "Living with a Short Sleep Gene: 'It's a Gift,'" CNN, June 22, 2021. www.cnn.com.

Elizabeth Weise, "Gene Found That Lets People Get By on 6 Hours of Sleep," ABC News, August 13, 2009. http://abcnews.go.com.

The results of the study revealed stark contrasts in sleeping situations among different groups of Americans. Only 32 percent of the participants said that they regularly got satisfying, restful sleep consisting of seven hours or more per night. In contrast, 33 percent of those surveyed—representing some 84 million people in the general population—reported getting less than seven hours of slumber and described their sleep situation as fair or poor. "Think getting six hours of sleep is enough?" ask sleep expert Melinda Smith and her colleagues at the online health site HelpGuide. "Think again," they answer. "In today's fast-paced society," they continue, six hours of sleep "may sound pretty good. In reality, though, it's a recipe for chronic sleep deprivation."[8]

Mental and Physical Complications

Smith and other sleep specialists point out that it is rarely a mystery that someone is chronically sleep deprived. Indeed, certain physical symptoms inevitably present themselves, although the

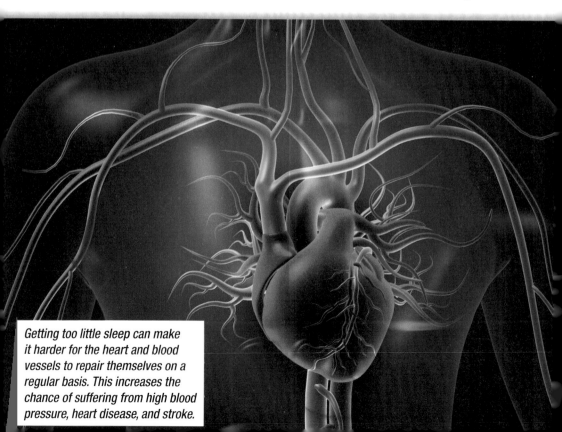

Getting too little sleep can make it harder for the heart and blood vessels to repair themselves on a regular basis. This increases the chance of suffering from high blood pressure, heart disease, and stroke.

Messing Up Our Internal Clock

In explaining the mechanics of sleeping, scientists often mention the circadian rhythm. This so-called biological clock consists of an internal twenty-four-hour cycle of wakefulness and sleep that responds to natural changes in light and darkness. Medical writers Brett and Kate McKay point out that although the circadian rhythm helps regulate a person's sleep cycles, it is often disrupted by outside factors. Medical experts call these factors *zeitgebers*, a German word meaning "time givers." The most influential zeitgeber is light. The McKays explain:

> When we're exposed to light, our brain produces more hormones, like serotonin, that make us feel awake; when it starts to get dark, our brain starts ramping up the sleepy hormone melatonin. The creation of artificial lights . . . [has] been blamed for messing up natural sleep cycles. While exposure to any kind of light can affect circadian rhythms . . . light with blue wavelengths is the most disruptive to melatonin production. Unfortunately, most of us put electronic devices right in front of our faces every night that primarily emit this blue light. If you've been having trouble falling asleep, it may be because you're . . . looking through Instagram photos on your smartphone late at night.

Brett McKay and Kate McKay, "What Every Man Should Know About Sleep," Art of Manliness, June 1, 2021. www.artofmanliness.com.

exact symptoms and the intensity of them can vary from person to person. Among them are feeling irritable or moody, having periodic bouts of daytime weariness or exhaustion, lacking the motivation to accomplish activities that used to be standard for the person, catching colds more easily and more often than in the past, being less creative and less able to solve problems than in the past, and finding it more difficult to deal with stress. A sleep-deprived person may also have trouble concentrating and remembering things. Unusual weight gain can be another symptom of long-term sleep deficits.

Underlying these and similar symptoms are mental and physical problems that, sleep scientists have found, can develop as a result of built-up sleep debt and chronic sleep deprivation. Some are related to the fact that sleep helps the brain form new cellular pathways that aid in learning and forming memories. A long-term sleep deficit can negatively affect one's memory. It can also make it more difficult to make simple daily decisions. In addition, it may become harder to concentrate and to control one's temper.

Physical health can also be impacted by sleep deprivation. For example, getting sufficient sleep helps maintain normal functions of various parts of the body, including the cardiovascular system, which includes the heart and blood vessels. Getting too little sleep can make it harder for those vessels to repair themselves on a regular basis. The chances of suffering from high blood pressure, heart disease, stroke, and diabetes are also higher for people who accumulate a lot of sleep debt.

Still another unhealthy side effect of a chronic lack of sleep is weight gain and obesity. In Hawker's words, "Research shows that poor sleep can disrupt hormones that regulate feelings of hunger and fullness. Sleeping well can help you manage food intake and control your weight."[9]

Indeed, sleep researchers have found that it is quite common for people to eat more when they are tired. This is not mere co-incidence, says neuroscientist and psychologist Matthew Walker. He explains, "Too little sleep swells concentrations of a hormone that makes you feel hungry while suppressing a companion hormone that otherwise signals food satisfaction. Despite being full, you still want to eat more. It's a proven recipe for weight gain in sleep-deficient adults and children alike."[10]

For these and other reasons, therefore, a prolonged lack of sleep can cause a reduction, either small or large, in a person's overall health. As Walker notes, "Evolution did not make a spectacular blunder in conceiving of sleep. Sleep dispenses a multitude of health-ensuring benefits, yours to pick up in repeat [doses] every twenty-four hours should you choose [to do so]."[11]

Chapter Two

Why Is Too Little Sleep So Common?

"The worst thing in the world is to try to sleep and not to,"[12] American writer F. Scott Fitzgerald, author of the iconic novel *The Great Gatsby*, once wrote. Millions of Americans, and millions more people around the world, would heartily agree with that statement. One of their number was the late Greenfield, Massachusetts, radio host Phil G. Vincent, who remarked:

> I've been suffering from insomnia my whole adult life. I've tried every pill and other so-called treatments or cures known to modern medicine, but most don't do very much. And I've had to learn to live with the fact that, like it or not, each day I'm going to feel and act like a zombie in the daylight hours, especially in late afternoons. It's a nightmare, but unfortunately not the kind you have when you're asleep![13]

Numerous recent studies have revealed that literally millions of Americans share Vincent's experiences with and frustrations about a chronic lack of sleep. A 2022 study by the Norwegian health organization Helsestart, for example, found that almost 50 percent of US adults have trouble sleeping at least once a month. The same study showed that 36 percent of American adults fight hard to fall asleep at least once a week and that 22 percent undergo the same struggle every night.

Other recent major sleep studies have corroborated this disturbing finding, producing similar alarming figures related to widespread lack of sleep. For instance, the CDC-sponsored National Health and Nutrition Examination Survey, conducted from 2017 to 2020, examined sleep data on more than nine thousand Americans age twenty and older. It found that close to 30 percent of Americans often have trouble falling or staying asleep most nights, and roughly 27 percent have bouts of drowsiness during the day on most days. In addition, this survey discovered, at least 10 percent of adults accumulate a sleep debt of at least two hours nearly every night.

Generalized Insomnia and Its Symptoms

Ordinary people and researchers alike regularly use the term *insomnia* to describe the cause of frequent sleeplessness. Technically speaking, insomnia is a specific sleep disorder with its own characteristic symptoms. But over the course of the past century, the term came to be widely used in a more general sense to denote the overall condition of having trouble sleeping. Indeed, Rachel Y. Moon, explains, insomnia has become "a broad term used to describe a wide range of complaints relating to sleep. These include decreased sleep quality or quantity, trouble *getting* to sleep, and trouble *maintaining* sleep."[14]

Using *insomnia* in this generalized way, sleep experts have compiled a list of typical symptoms and triggers for these all-too-common sleep troubles. In addition to frequent difficulty falling asleep, a recurrent symptom consists of the person finally achieving a state of slumber but then waking up two or more times during the night. He or she is also prone to rising from bed the next morning earlier than necessary. That person habitually feels drowsy on and off as the day proceeds. Nancy Foldvary-Schaefer, director of the Sleep Disorders Center at the well-known Cleveland Clinic, notes other common symptoms of insomnia. "Are you a worrywart?" she asks. "Does your mind race at night? Do you spend the nighttime hours thinking about your problems, the next day's schedule, or worries about sleep loss? Do you experience increased muscle tension or agitation . . . or inability to relax at night?"[15] All of these conditions are common in people who experience insomnia.

Insomnia is not the same in all people, however. An undetermined number of people experience a heightened form of sleep loss known as psychophysiological insomnia. Its symptoms begin with the person feeling a lot of stress, which makes it difficult to get to sleep. As time goes on, he or she develops a fear or dread of not being able to sleep normally. That only increases the stress, which makes the insomnia even worse, and as Foldvary-Schaefer says, "a vicious cycle develops,"[16] in which bedtime becomes the main focus of tension in that person's life.

Stress, Depression, and Pain

Stress, it turns out, plays a major role not only in extreme forms of insomnia but also in many of the other examples of sleep deprivation that plague society. The causes of such stress are numerous. They can include tension between parents and children or between husband and wife, divorce, serious money troubles, prolonged illness, trouble with the law, the death of a loved one, and the loss of one's job, among others. Any one of these, or a combination of two or more, can make it hard for someone to sleep.

In studying these common triggers of sleep loss, scientists have learned how the stress they cause manifests itself in the brain, especially in relation to the processes that are important in regulating sleep. "Unmanaged daily stress," says Colorado-based sleep expert Herbert Ross, "can deplete your hormonal and nutrient reserves." Moreover, he adds, various unresolved emotional or psychological issues "can disturb brain chemistry and [thereby] hinder deep sleep."[17]

Besides stress, one of the most common causes of sleep problems in modern society is clinical depression, a condition in which a person feels helpless and hopeless about life. He or she typically loses interest in most daily activities, feels lonely or useless, exhibits low energy levels, and may seek comfort in increased use of alcohol or drugs. Not surprisingly, clinical depression also frequently interferes with normal sleep patterns. In fact, a depressed person may end up sleeping either too little or too much. On the one hand,

Tricked by Artificial Light

Although the blue light emitted by computer and cell phone screens is particularly detrimental to people's attempts to fall asleep, it is important to emphasize that almost any kind of light has a similar, though less intense, effect. As Matthew Walker, a professor of neuroscience at the University of California, Berkeley, explains, the invention of electric lights in the late 1800s

> redefined the meaning of midnight for generations thereafter. Artificial evening light, even that of modest strength . . . will fool your suprachiasmatic nucleus into believing the sun has not yet set. . . . The artificial light that bathes our modern indoor worlds will therefore halt the forward progress of biological time that is normally signaled by the evening surge of the [natural, sleep-inducing hormone] melatonin. Sleep in modern humans is delayed from taking off the evening runway, which would naturally occur somewhere between 8 and 10 p.m., just as we observe in hunter-gatherer tribes. Artificial light in modern societies thus tricks us into believing night is still day.

Matthew Walker, *Why We Sleep: Unlocking the Power of Sleep and Dreams*. New York: Scribner, 2017, p. 267.

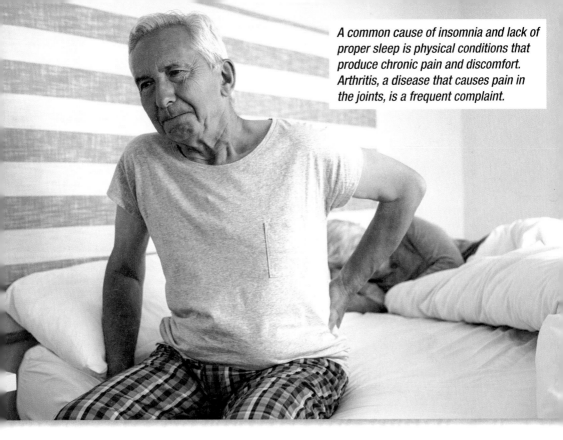

A common cause of insomnia and lack of proper sleep is physical conditions that produce chronic pain and discomfort. Arthritis, a disease that causes pain in the joints, is a frequent complaint.

Moon explains, if that individual does not sleep enough, he or she may feel "exhausted during the day, and may face each succeeding night with increasing anxiety about not getting [enough] sleep. . . . [Yet] depression can also lead a person to sleep many more hours than usual and wake up feeling groggy, tired, and still depressed."[18]

Other common causes of insomnia and lack of proper sleep are physical conditions that produce chronic pain and discomfort. Arthritis, a disease that causes pain in the joints, is a notable example. So is chronic heartburn, or gastric reflux disease, which causes repeated burning sensations in the esophagus. Ailments that make it hard for a person to breathe normally— such as asthma—constitute other typical examples of conditions that make sleeping difficult.

Stimulants and Depressants

No less common than pain and discomfort in the general population is the widespread use of various chemical substances. One of the most familiar and prevalent is the stimulant caffeine, a key ingredient in coffee, tea, chocolate, and many kinds of soft drinks. Although when consumed in moderate amounts, caffeine is only mildly addictive, it does make getting to sleep harder and can stay in a person's system for up to ten hours. Therefore, experts warn, one should avoid ingesting that substance after early afternoon.

Far more addictive is the stimulant nicotine, found in tobacco products. As Petra Hawker of the London Sleep Centre states, "Smokers take longer to fall asleep, sleep for an average of 33 minutes less every night, and sleep more lightly than nonsmokers. The best advice is to avoid nicotine. Withdrawing from nicotine can make your sleep worse, but this effect is short-lived."[19]

Other substances that tend to be used habitually and that negatively affect sleep are depressants. By far the most common one is alcohol. It significantly reduces the amount of REM sleep a person gets, making it more likely that he or she will awaken feeling tired or sluggish. Alcohol is also a diuretic, which means that it can make someone get up once or more in the middle of the night to urinate, thereby further interfering with sleep.

Social Jet Lag

Stress, depression, arthritis, drinking alcohol, and so forth all deal with personal feelings, conditions, and habits. Much more communal in nature and broader in scope is difficulty sleeping based on the fast pace of modern society and people's struggles to keep up with and succeed within it. Sleep researchers often call this *social jet lag*. In a nutshell, society has a sort of fast-moving clock that drives the pace of life. That societal clock frequently conflicts with people's personal, inner biological clocks, which demand a certain amount of sleep each day. "The timing of your sleep on workdays," says Dr. Elizabeth Klerman, a professor of neurology at Harvard Medical School in Boston, is driven by "societal and work con-

Alcohol significantly reduces the amount of REM sleep a person gets, making it more likely that he or she will awaken feeling tired or sluggish.

straints. But the timing of your sleep on free days is what your body clock really wants you to do." When the two clocks clash, she goes on, "it's like you're living in a state of jet lag during the work week."[20]

This conclusion was borne out in the CDC's National Health and Nutrition Examination Survey. More than 46 percent of the participants said they estimated they experienced at least one hour of social jet lag per day. Another 19 percent approximated their daily lag time at two or more hours. After reading the study, California-based sleep specialist Dr. Raj Dasgupta remarked, "With strict work schedules and jam-packed weekend activities, it's not surprising that many individuals report that their sleep needs are not being met during the week."[21] He confirms that, left untreated, social jet lag can cause daytime fatigue, difficulty concentrating, and depression and can contribute to obesity and diabetes.

Unusually Sensitive to Blue Light

Combining both personal and societal elements is a phenomenon that has, for tens of millions of people worldwide, become increasingly detrimental to falling asleep. It consists of the pervasive, almost universal use of electronic media, especially computers and cell phones. Rob Newsom, of the Seattle-based Sleep Foundation, summarizes the problem:

> Checking social media, sending emails, or looking at the news before bed can keep us awake, as nighttime use of electronics can affect sleep through the stimulating-effects of light from digital screens. While all light can interfere with our [inner clocks], the 24-hour internal rhythms that control processes like the sleep-wake cycle, the blue light emitted from electronic screens has the greatest impact on sleep. Blue light stimulates parts of the brain that make us feel alert, leaving us energized at bedtime when we should be winding down.[22]

The most crucial of the "parts of the brain" Newsom mentions is the suprachiasmatic nucleus. About the size of an acorn, it essentially serves as the body's biological pacemaker because it controls various natural rhythms, including a person's inner clock that regulates sleep cycles. Receptors within the eyes communicate with the suprachiasmatic nucleus, telling it that it is either daytime or nighttime. The problem is that those receptors are unusually sensitive to blue light, the very type of light emitted by computer and cell phone screens. So when a person uses such a device, his or her eyes in a sense loudly scream to the brain that it is daytime, even when it is not. And this makes it difficult for that individual to fall asleep.

The scope of this problem in modern society is massive. As Matthew Walker puts it, untold numbers of people around the globe stare directly at "laptop screens, smartphones, and tablets each night, sometimes for many hours, often

"Blue light stimulates parts of the brain that makes us feel alert, leaving us energized at bedtime when we should be winding down."[22]

—Rob Newsom of the Seattle-based Sleep Foundation

Little Sleep and Big Accomplishments

Over the centuries, a small number of prominent people claimed they could accomplish a lot on very little sleep. These individuals supposedly had a special gift that allowed them more time to accomplish brilliant tasks for the good of humanity. Among their number were Renaissance artist Leonardo da Vinci, French military general Napoleon Bonaparte, US founders Benjamin Franklin and Thomas Jefferson, and American inventor Thomas Edison. The latter claimed he got only two or three hours of sleep per night and sometimes worked on his inventions for seventy-two hours straight with no sleep at all. It turns out, however, that this claim was false. The reality was that Edison regularly took two or three morning and afternoon naps each day and hid that practice from all but a couple of coworkers. Indeed, modern sleep experts have concluded that the claims of prominent people who accomplish a lot on very little sleep are little more than myth.

with these devices just feet, or even inches away from [their] retinas."[23] Various studies indicate that at least 70 percent of those who own such electronic devices use them in bed shortly before trying to get to sleep. As a result, these individuals are far more likely to have trouble sleeping than those who do not use electronic media at bedtime.

Millions Often Half Awake?

Considering all these factors—from stress, caffeine consumption, and other personal factors, to social jet lag and blue light from electronic screens—it can be said with some confidence that the populations of many modern nations are seriously sleep deprived. And according to Sara Martin, director of the Nebraska-based Wellness Council of America, the United States is no exception. Indeed, she writes, "a quick check of the nation's pulse reveals that insomnia, in all its many forms, has become one more aspect on a growing list of national health epidemics." This troubling situation, Martin continues, which witnesses millions of people staggering through life often seemingly half awake, "gives a whole new meaning to the expression 'the coming zombie apocalypse.' Many would say it's already here!"[24]

Chapter Three

Sleep Loss in Young People

It is an alarming fact that young people (generally, early teens to midtwenties) in modern industrialized countries like the United States, Canada, and the United Kingdom get much less than the amount of sleep they require for optimum health. Even more concerning, 25 percent of Americans in their late teens and early twenties suffer from insomnia almost every night. According to psychotherapists and sleep specialists Heather Turgeon and Julie Wright:

> Modern-day teens are the most sleep-deprived group of any individuals the world has ever seen. While the majority of elementary school kids get the optimal amount of sleep most nights, that number drops to about 30 percent by middle-school, and by their senior year 5 percent of teens get optimal sleep on school nights. . . . A recent survey of sixty thousand American high school students measured how well teens are faring in terms of the basic health recommendations for sleep, screen use, and exercise. Only 3 percent of girls and 7 percent of boys reached those targets.[25]

Sounding the Alarm About Blue Light

Why do so many young people today get so little sleep? Time spent on digital devices is one big reason for this. According to a 2022 Pew Research Center report, 46 percent of teens surveyed say they almost constantly use the internet. Among the biggest draws are online platforms such as TikTok, YouTube, and Instagram. According to the same survey, 35 percent of teens say they are on at least one such platform almost all the time.

Staring at a screen for hours on end, especially at night, can disrupt sleep. Electronic devices such as cell phones and tablets emit blue light. Blue light is known to stimulate the brain and in doing so makes people feel alert and energized. This phenomenon has proved to be detrimental to adults' sleep, and thereby their health. It is potentially more harmful to young people because they spend so many hours online.

Matthew Walker, director of the University of California, Berkeley's Sleep and Neuroimaging Lab, has been a leader in sounding the alarm about the damaging effects of blue electronic light on sleep patterns, including those of young people. In his 2017 book on sleep, he describes how he has frequently seen children and teens staring directly at computer and cell phone screens at night, sometimes for hours at a time. "The devices are a wonderful piece of technology. They enrich the lives and education of our youth. But such technology is also enriching their eyes and brains with powerful blue light that has a damaging effect on sleep, the sleep that young, developing brains so desperately need in order to flourish."[26]

Impaired Motor Skills

When teens get too little sleep, the effects are more serious than just being tired the next day. One result involves impairment of basic motor skills. A number of studies of this problem have been done in multiple countries since the early 2000s. One such study, led by Dr. Mairav Cohen-Zion of Israel's Academic College of Tel Aviv-Yaffo, examined whether getting insufficient sleep during the night can impair adolescent students' execution of normal activities the next day. This research revealed that the students who

In a recent survey, 46 percent of teens say they almost constantly use the internet. Among the biggest draws are online platforms such as TikTok, YouTube, and Instagram.

got too little sleep had reduced motor skills, including hand-eye coordination, than young people who got sufficient sleep.

Cohen-Zion had expected the negative effects of sleep loss to be most pronounced when the young people tried to do complex tasks. But to her surprise, this was not the case. Even when the sleep-deprived youths tried to do the simplest of tasks, they periodically had trouble focusing. "They did badly," Cohen-Zion concludes, "because they were unchallenged and tired and didn't make an effort. Their attention flagged."[27]

School Start Times

Cohen-Zion's study confirmed the results of similar studies that Israeli researchers had performed in the roughly two decades preceding hers. Disturbed by these findings, many of that nation's educators had discussed ways to remedy the situation. Since they could not force the country's young people to go to bed earlier, they had recommended that school start times be delayed till a bit later in the morning. The hope was that this would allow students to get more sleep before attending classes. Although that approach has not yet been instituted throughout Israel, some of the country's school districts are experimenting with it.

Meanwhile, in the United States one recent experiment of this type began in Colorado in the fall of 2022. In the Cherry Creek School District near Denver, officials moved high school start times from 7:10 a.m. to 8:20 a.m. and middle school start times from 8:00 a.m. to 8:50 a.m. The initial results were extremely positive, said Colorado-based psychologist and sleep researcher Lisa Meltzer. She told local newspaper and TV reporters:

> By delaying both middle school and high school start times, what we found is that the students were sleeping later which meant they were sleeping longer. Their bedtimes did not significantly change, but their wake times did. It's very important. Not just for sleep, but also for engagement, for the ability for students to be alert, especially in the morning. Parents reported significant changes in their teenagers, in particular their mood. They are described as no longer being zombies in the morning. The students described the benefits of being able to go to school when the sun was up and not when it was dark out.[28]

Efforts like these are under way in other states as well. In California in 2019 state lawmakers passed a law requiring the state's school districts to push back start times beginning in the fall of 2022. The law requires all high schools to start no earlier than 8:30 a.m. The law also states that middle schools must not start before 8:00 a.m.

Local California newspapers and television stations interviewed dozens of students and their parents in October 2022, weeks after the changes went into effect, to get feedback on the new start times. Most of those interviewed liked the changes. One thirteen-year-old boy said he no longer felt greatly rushed

Studies based on moving school start times to an hour later in the morning to allow students to get more sleep have shown positive results. Students were found to be more alert and focused during classes.

and overly tired each morning while getting ready for school. His mother also praised the changes, remarking that her son no longer acted like a zombie after she awakened him each morning.

Another mother explained that her son has epilepsy and that he tends to have seizures if he does not get enough sleep. Before the new law went into effect, she said, he periodically had early morning seizures. But with the changes, she went on, he now gets enough sleep to make morning seizures quite rare.

Overextended Teens

As helpful as later school start times appear to be, these changes do not address one of the chief causes of too little sleep among youth. Over the years, researchers have found that many young people take on too many activities or have too many responsibilities. By overextending themselves, many teens experience exhaustion and increased stress. This in turn can negatively affect their physical and mental health. Eric Suni of the widely respected Sleep Foundation (formerly the National Sleep Foundation) describes a common scenario for many teens:

Teens often have their hands full. School assignments, work obligations, household chores, social life, community activities, and sports are just some of the things that can require their time and attention. With so much to try to fit into each day, many teens don't allocate sufficient time for sleep. They may stay up late during the week to finish homework or during the weekend when hanging out with friends, both of which can reinforce their night owl schedule.[29]

Some young people are well aware of the danger of becoming overextended in middle school, high school, and college. "If you're asking yourself whether or not you have too many extracurriculars, chances are you *might* have a bit too much on your plate," one nineteen-year-old Columbia University student blogged in 2018. Such activities can be both enriching and fun. "If you are getting sick or constantly feeling overwhelmed and stressed out, however," she added, "then this may be a sign that it's time to start dialing back your extracurricular activities. . . . Spreading yourself too thin will only end up creating more problems for you. You might end up getting seriously ill or burning out."[30]

Young people who do spread themselves too thin often experience heightened stress as they try to manage all of their activities and responsibilities. Stress is a well-known cause of disrupted sleep, and disrupted sleep can lead to more stress. This is true for both teens and adults. "It's a vicious circle," says Harvard Medical School researcher Dr. Edward Pace-Schott. "The more stressed you get," he explains, "the less you sleep, and the less you sleep, the more stressed you get. And in the long term, that can lead to serious psychiatric problems,"[31] such as clinical depression or general anxiety disorder.

> "The more stressed you get, the less you sleep, and the less you sleep, the more stressed you get."[31]
>
> —Dr. Edward Pace-Schott, Harvard Medical School researcher

Playing Catch-Up

Studies of and interviews with middle school, high school, and college students indicate that most young people in those categories realize they should be getting more sleep than they do. The question is, what are they prepared to do about it? To date, bedtimes for most people in this general age group have not changed in at least two decades. Overall, young people still stay up a good deal later than they did in previous generations.

By contrast, one approach many students *do* take on and off is an attempt to make up for their weekday sleep deficits by trying to get more sleep on the weekends. Unfortunately for those who take this path, it largely does not work. As George Washington University medical professor Rachel Moon puts it:

> Trying to "catch up" on weekends is a problem for a number of reasons. First, it does not help performance during the school week. Second, the weekend shift in bedtimes and wake times tends to exacerbate the normal adolescent sleep/wake delay. This results in a situation similar to chronic jet lag, as the teen struggles to shift her sleep patterns back and forth. Some of these teens even develop a sleep disorder called delayed sleep phase, in which the biological shift in sleep patterns becomes even more pronounced, leading to extreme difficulty falling asleep and waking up at the desired times.[32]

The fact that young people as a whole are not making up for their weekday sleep deficits on weekends, or most other times, can be seen in statistics revealed in repeated studies. According to data released by the Sleep Foundation in 2022, for example, some 70 percent of US teens get less sleep than they should, and fewer than 10 percent get the amount of sleep recommended by sleep scientists. Moreover, an estimated 27 percent are at risk of developing depression and other psychiatric problems.

Depression

Indeed, regarding teens who suffer from depression, a 2019 study conducted by University of Minnesota sleep researcher Rachel Widome and her colleagues highlighted the troubling scope of the problem. The study demonstrated that one in three young people who sleep fewer than six hours each night for weeks on end will begin showing classic symptoms of depression. In comparison, Widome reports, only one in ten students who do get enough sleep each night tend to show any depressive symptoms.

This problem with teenage depression caused by sleep deprivation did not appear suddenly, Widome says. Rather, it happened fairly gradually, over a decade or two. She blames a combination of factors, all related to the steadily changing habits of young people in society. Teens now spend far more time using computers, cell phones, video games, and the like than they did even ten or fifteen years ago. Moreover, much of that use of electronic devices occurs in the evening, when young people should be winding down to go to bed. Widome also cites the increased

Video Gamers and Sleep

After video games became a widespread pastime among young people in the 1990s, sleep scientists suspected that playing those games for hours each day must affect players' sleep habits. In particular, researchers worried that playing video games at night might be problematic. This was found to be true by a series of studies conducted from 2010 to 2019 by sleep researchers at Flinders University in Adelaide, Australia. Surveys sponsored by the Sleep Foundation from 2019 to 2022 confirmed these findings. First, the researchers found that the longer individuals play video games in the evening hours, the more they push back their bedtimes. Specifically, for each thirty minutes a young person plays a game, he or she stays up an additional sixteen minutes. Another conclusion of the studies was that playing these games pulls users into a "flow state," or extremely strong desire to continue playing, which further extends the playing session. According to clinical psychologist and sleep expert Michael J. Breus, "People lose track of time when they game. If you're having a bad game *or* doing really well, you keep [playing]. That's not what you need to be doing within 90 minutes before bed."

Quoted in Lauren Gravitz, "How Gamers Actually Sleep," Sleep Foundation, November 18, 2022. www.sleepfoundation.org.

marketing of caffeinated drinks to young people in the past two decades.

Not only do these actions cause young people to sleep less and become more depressed, Widome states, but they also appear to lay the foundation for depression and other psychiatric problems later in life. Her study found that students who did not get enough sleep when they were in the tenth and eleventh grades consistently showed various symptoms of depression in their early and midtwenties.

Health and Well-Being

These findings and those in many similar recent studies worry the experts. They hope to reach an increasing number of young people with the facts about the extreme importance of getting proper amounts of sleep in their lives. One of the more crucial of these facts is the well-established connection between sleep and memory, since a good memory is an essential aid to students of all ages. Pace-Schott points out, "Study results show better

A recent study demonstrated that one in three young people who sleep fewer than six hours each night for weeks on end will begin showing classic symptoms of depression.

How YouTube Affects Young People's Sleep

It turns out that the effects on young people's brains of watching television, reading words on a computer screen, and watching videos on YouTube are not all the same. Scientists say that watching YouTube is the most detrimental of those activities to teens' ability to get enough sleep. This was the finding of an Australian study published in the December 2022 issue of the scientific journal *Sleep Medicine*. "We wanted to learn if there were specific apps that people should avoid, so that they could continue using their devices in a healthy way that didn't affect sleep," recalls one of the study's co-authors, Michael Gradisar. "We've been seeing teenagers who have sleep problems in our clinic. . . . Many of them mentioned that they would watch YouTube as they try to fall asleep."

After having the teen test subjects use several different apps at bedtime multiple times, Gradisar states, he and his colleagues found that YouTube was the only app that consistently and harmfully affected the young subjects' sleep. For every fifteen minutes of YouTube teens watched, the study found, they displayed a 24 percent greater chance of getting fewer than seven hours of shut-eye.

Quoted in Cara Murez, "One App Is Especially Bad for Teens' Sleep," *U.S. News & World Report*, September 13, 2022. www.usnews.com.

performance if you learn material and then sleep on it, instead of remaining awake. So there's lots and lots of evidence now indicating that sleep promotes memory strengthening and memory consolidation."[33]

Eric Suni sums up some other key points of the argument for young people building better sleep habits, saying that "students who sleep better enjoy better [mood] and [overall] better health." Furthermore, he continues, it is likely impossible to find a young person anywhere who does not want to make higher scores and grades in school. And the fact is that healthy sleep is directly associated with higher grade point averages. So it makes sense, he tells students, to get more sleep because "your grades will thank you for it!"[34]

Chapter Four

The Hazards of Getting Too Little Sleep

In early 2015, newspapers in the region of DeWitt, New York (near the city of Syracuse), reported on a tragedy in a local nursing home. A thirty-five-year-old nurse was charged with gross neglect after the death of a twenty-five-year-old man who was bedridden in the home. Her task, during a twelve-hour shift, local police said, was to check on the young man every two hours to make sure he was getting enough oxygen. However, she fell asleep on the job and failed to check on her patient for almost eight hours. As a result, he suffered brain damage and died two weeks later. The nurse was later found guilty of endangering the life of a disabled person and sentenced to ninety days in jail.

Workplaces of All Kinds Affected

In the weeks that followed, media commentators pointed out that such incidents are not unusual. Statistics show that falling asleep on the job occurs in workplaces of all kinds, from hospitals to factories to retail stores to offices to construction sites. The number of deaths caused by fatigue in the workplace is unknown. But the Occupational Safety and Health Administration (OSHA) and the National Safety Council offer a rough estimate of the number of injuries caused by falling asleep at work. Of the 7 million workplace injuries that happen annually in the country, these organizations say, approximately 13 percent appear to be related to tired workers who doze off on the job. That works out to a bit over nine hundred thousand workplace injuries per year attributable to drowsiness. What is more, OSHA estimates that these accidents and injuries cause productivity losses of roughly $136 billion per year in the United States.

According to OSHA and the National Academy of Medicine, of the many kinds of workplaces affected by sleepy employees, hospitals are especially open to potentially serious harm. According to Anju Khanna Saggi of the online site Sleep Cycle:

> Lack of sleep can not only affect a physician's mood, exposing patients and hospitals to negative emotions, such as tension, hostility, and confusion greatly affecting patient care. Patient safety is also affected, with the [National Academy of Medicine] revealing that medical errors cause between 44,000–98,000 deaths a year. And although it's difficult to pinpoint the number that is directly caused by sleep-deprived healthcare professionals, it is assumed to be a likely contributor.[35]

Those disturbing figures count only the incidents in which medical workers or patients endured some sort of physical harm. Experts point out that thousands of incidents in which someone falls asleep at work without anyone getting hurt happen all the time. In many of these cases, luck or skill can be credited with preventing disaster. One such incident took place in March 2011 at the Ronald Reagan Washington National Airport in Arlington, Virginia. An air traffic controller—the only one on duty that evening—fell fast asleep at his desk. In the minutes that followed, two incoming airliners routinely radioed the tower to seek assistance to land. When repeated requests went unanswered, the pilots had to land without guidance. Fortunately for all involved, their skill and composure saved the day, and no tragedy occurred.

Statistics show that falling asleep on the job occurs in workplaces of all kinds. Of the 7 million workplace injuries that happen annually in the United States, approximately 13 percent appear to be related to tired workers who doze off on the job.

Sleep Deprivation–Caused Problems

Organizations that do research on sleep agree it is not surprising that sleep-related workplace incidents occur so frequently. Studies by the Sleep Foundation, for instance, reveal that sleep-deprived people are about 70 percent more likely to have accidents at work than those who get sufficient sleep. One crucial question that the sleep researchers regularly try to answer is, why does a chronic lack of sleep make it more likely for workers to make mistakes or have accidents on the job; that is, what are the primary problems caused by sleep deprivation?

First, the experts point out, chronic sleep loss causes impaired motor skills, including hand-eye coordination, depth perception, and balance. "This is especially dangerous for construction workers who risk falling when balancing on ladders or walking on scaffolding," says Gina Wynn of the biotech research company Fisher Scientific. Poor decision-making and increased likelihood of taking risks are also problems linked to getting too little sleep, she states.

"Lack of sleep can alter a person's judgment and leads to riskier behavior like failing to wear personal protective equipment due to discomfort. Oftentimes people don't even realize they are compromised. For healthcare workers, OSHA cites increased errors in patient care and occupational injuries, including needle-sticks and exposure to blood and other body fluids."[36]

In addition, people with chronic sleep loss cause workplace accidents because their memory and information-processing abilities are impaired to one degree or another. On the job, they are less able to focus on individual tasks and to retain new information. As a result, even small distractions can lead them to make costly mistakes that can become safety hazards.

An inability to deal with normal stresses associated with a given job or profession can also be a by-product of repeatedly getting too little sleep. This can affect people emotionally, Wynn

More Accidents Due to Daylight Saving Time?

According to the Occupational Safety and Health Administration (OSHA), the loss of an hour that occurs each spring when daylight saving time begins can be problematic. Data collected by OSHA over the years shows that, thanks to that time change, many people get almost an hour less sleep each night for roughly a week until their bodies adjust to the change. An OSHA spokesperson explains, "It can take about one week for the body to adjust to the new times for sleeping, eating, and activity. Until they have adjusted, people can have trouble falling asleep, staying asleep, and waking up at the right time. This can lead to sleep deprivation and reduction in performance, increasing the risk for mistakes." As a result, OSHA reports, workplace injuries increase by almost 6 percent during that transitional period. Moreover, overall, the injuries tend to be more severe. OSHA therefore recommends that employers alert their workers to this problem. They should, the agency states, "remind workers to be especially vigilant while driving, at work, and at home to protect themselves since others around them may be sleepier and at risk for making an error that can cause a vehicle crash or other accident."

Occupational Safety and Health Administration, "Workplace Injuries Increase After Time Change." https://osha10hrtraining.com.

explains. "It can make them irritable and prone to outbursts that can reduce productivity. Sleep deprivation may cause anxiety, depression, and lack of motivation. In turn, stress and emotional turbulence can . . . lead to further risk of having an accident at work."[37]

A Major Cause of Traffic Accidents

These same sorts of diminished capacities—impaired motor skills, inability to focus, poor judgment, and so forth—are major factors in another kind of mishap frequently caused by chronic sleep loss—traffic accidents. Indeed, so-called drowsy driving is one of the main causes of such accidents on a year-to-year basis. The National Safety Council, which keeps track of these incidents, estimates that falling asleep at the wheel, or almost doing so, causes around one hundred thousand car and truck crashes annually. Of these, roughly fifteen hundred result in at least one fatality, and about seventy thousand produce injuries of one type or another.

It is estimated that falling asleep while driving causes one hundred thousand car and truck crashes annually. Of these, roughly fifteen hundred result in at least one fatality.

Other statistics about drowsy driving have been collected by the Foundation for Traffic Safety (FTS), a division of the American Automobile Association. For instance, the FTS reports, each year driver fatigue is a contributing factor in almost 10 percent of all US car and truck crashes. Also, drowsiness is a factor in close to 11 percent of crashes involving injury or significant property damage.

Complicating matters, the FTS points out, is that it is often very difficult for police and other authorities to determine whether drowsy driving has been a factor in a crash. "Unlike impairment by substances such as alcohol," the FTS states,

> there is no test analogous to a breathalyzer that the police can administer at the roadside to assess a driver's level of drowsiness at or shortly after the time of a crash. More-over, a driver who was drowsy before a crash may appear fully alert afterward and may be reluctant to volunteer to the police that he or she was drowsy. In the case of a driv-er who was not actually asleep at the time of the crash but was operating at a reduced level of alertness, the driver may not even recognize that he or she was drowsy.[38]

Young People and Drowsy Driving

According to the FTS, this uncertainty factor means that the ac-tual proportion of crashes caused by drowsy driving is likely a good deal higher than the official estimate of about 10 percent. Whatever the actual number of those mishaps may be, experts say, it appears that young people are responsible for many of them. In fact, the National Safety Council estimates that a whop-ping 50 percent or more of those incidents involve drivers below age twenty-five.

That reality seriously bothered seventeen-year-old Talia M. Dunietz of Ann Arbor, Michigan. Drowsy driving had not been addressed in her driver's education classes. And when she ex-pressed her concerns in a short essay and sent it to the American

Academy of Sleep Medicine, it printed the piece on its website. The essay, which the academy fact-checked for accuracy, states in part:

> As a high school student, I am familiar with sleep deprivation and the constant need to balance schoolwork, extracurriculars, and social activities. As a new driver, I am aware of the risks of drunk driving, but drowsy driving was never on my radar. On school days I leave the house at 7:20 a.m. (often sleep deprived) and drive a short distance to school. A rarely discussed topic, driving while sleepy has almost as high of a risk as driving while drunk. . . . As the amount of alcohol consumption increases, the risk of crashes becomes higher. Sleep deprivation has similar effects on the brain. Teens are taught to avoid driving after drinking; why not teach them to avoid driving while sleepy?[39]

Fatigue in Other Kinds of Crashes

Cars and trucks are not the only vehicles in which drowsiness can lead to tragedy. Trains and airplanes are similarly vulnerable to crashes when workers fall asleep on the job. No one knows for sure how many train crashes have occurred over the past century or so as a result of engineers succumbing to the effects of drowsiness. But people who work in the transportation industry say it is far from rare. "The rail business is an industry full of tired, stressed workers," said former railroad trainmaster Georgetta Gregory in March 2016. She knew this firsthand, she stated, because she had been one of those stressed workers. She recalled, "The job was very stressful and required long hours. It wasn't unusual for me to work 80 hours a week . . . [and] over time I became chronically

"As a new driver, I am aware of the risks of drunk driving, but drowsy driving was never on my radar."[39]

—Talia M. Dunietz, a seventeen-year-old in Ann Arbor, Michigan

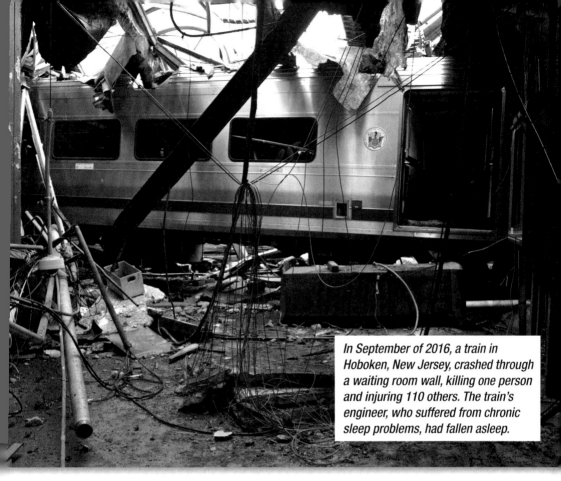

In September of 2016, a train in Hoboken, New Jersey, crashed through a waiting room wall, killing one person and injuring 110 others. The train's engineer, who suffered from chronic sleep problems, had fallen asleep.

fatigued. . . . Eventually, I began to make mistakes at work and in my personal life—potentially dangerous ones. . . . I warned my bosses, but there was little help or response."[40]

In September 2016, only a few months after Gregory issued her warning, one of the more serious train crashes of recent times occurred in Hoboken, New Jersey. A passenger train nearing the local station failed to slow down and stop and plowed through a wall of the building's waiting room, killing one person and injuring 110 others. After investigating the disaster, the National Transportation Safety Board said that the engineer, who suffered from chronic sleep problems, had dozed off as the train neared the station.

Severe drowsiness was also the cause of one of the worst airliner crashes of the early twenty-first century. On June 1, 2009, an Air France flight en route to Paris from Brazil was in the fourth hour of the flight. Unknown to the passengers, the craft's captain had gotten only one hour of sleep the night before, and his two copilots had gotten only two or three hours each. The trouble began when the plane suddenly encountered a band of heavy thunderstorms. The turbulence was unusually severe, and the reaction times of the overtired pilots were too slow, resulting in their losing control of the aircraft. The men struggled to stabilize it, but to no avail. The plane lost power, spiraled downward, and crashed, killing all 228 passengers and crew on impact.

Often an Unpleasant Price to Pay

Large-scale accidents sometimes caused by lack of sleep, like train and plane crashes, naturally capture much media attention. Far less known to the public are personal sleep-related mishaps that happen in the home and most often involve a single individual. Sleep experts point out that too little sleep significantly increases the risk of falling and injury.

Particularly vulnerable to such domestic accidents are elderly and infirm people, either in private houses or nursing homes. According to Dr. Phyllis C. Zee, director of the Sleep Disorders Center at Northwestern Memorial Hospital in Chicago, "In older people, there are multiple mental and physical factors that,

Metro-North's Deadliest Crash

The 2016 Hoboken, New Jersey, train crash occurred only a little over two years after a similar calamity that had proved to be the single-deadliest crash in the history of New York's busy Metro-North Railroad. On the morning of December 1, 2013, the Metro-North train was passing through New York City. As it neared a sharp turn, where normally it slowed down considerably, the engineer fell asleep, and the locomotive's untended controls sped it up to 82 miles per hour (132 kph). Almost three times the posted speed limit for the turn, this was far too fast to allow the train to stay on the tracks, and it suddenly derailed. All seven passenger cars careened sideways, causing tree limbs, rocks, and other debris to smash inward through the windows. Four people were killed almost instantly, and another sixty-one were injured, some seriously. Dozens of police officers and 125 New York City firefighters rushed to the crash scene to give aid. Later, it was determined that the crash, caused by one man's extreme fatigue, did over $9 million worth of damage.

when combined with insomnia, can lead to falls."[41]

Whether an accident occurs at home, at work, on a highway, or on a train or airplane, says Brian C. Tefft of the FTS, sleep deprivation does not discriminate among

victims, places, or times. The fact is that everyone requires sleep on a regular basis, and if they get too little of it, there is often an unpleasant price to pay. Tefft frequently reminds people that "being awake isn't the same as being alert. [And] falling asleep isn't the only risk. Even if they manage to stay awake, sleep-deprived [people] are still at increased risk of making mistakes—like failing to notice something important . . . which can have tragic consequences."[42]

Chapter Five

How to Get More and Better Sleep

"You wake up to the alarm on your phone and reach over to turn it off," says sleep expert and sports coach Nick Littlehales.

> While you're there, you check the notifications beamed in overnight from your news, sports, and entertainment feeds, your social media apps, and emails and texts from work and friends. Your mouth is dry, your head is already spinning with what's to come this morning, the curtains are leaking light, and [a] light on the TV at the foot of the bed is staring unblinkingly at you. . . . Welcome to your day. Did you sleep well? Do you know *how* to sleep well?[43]

There was a day when Littlehales would have had to answer that question with a decided *no*. But after he entered the fast-growing field of sleep science, he steadily but surely learned both how absolutely crucial sleep is and how to make sure to get enough to maintain a healthy life. At least, he discovered the best sleep strategy that worked for *him*. He also learned that what worked for him did not necessarily work as well for others. Indeed, he and his colleagues now know that differences in people's backgrounds, personalities, professions, and living conditions dictate varied strategies and approaches to building good sleep habits.

Finding the right strategy can require learning through trial and error. By "trying out a variety of healthy sleep-promoting techniques," sleep specialist Melinda Smith says, "you can discover your personal prescription to a good night's rest. The key is to experiment. What works for some might not work as well for others. It's important to find the sleep strategies that work best for you."[44]

Basics of Good Sleep Hygiene

Sleep experts like Littlehales and Smith explain that whichever sleep strategy a person may adopt, it should contain most of the basics of what has come to be called "good sleep hygiene." Another authority on the subject, Petra Hawker, defines good sleep hygiene as "developing helpful, healthy sleep habits and sticking to them." Perhaps the most fundamental of all those habits, she notes, is to sustain a consistent sleep schedule—or put another way, to maintain regular periods of sleep on a daily basis. "Going to sleep and waking up at the same time every day," she writes, "is the most effective way to keep your internal body clock on an even keel."[45]

Another sleep hygiene basic pertains to taking naps. For some people a short nap reduces fatigue, improves mood, and offers relaxation. For others, napping leads to daytime grogginess and trouble sleeping. To benefit from napping, the Mayo Clinic recommends keeping naps short—about ten to twenty minutes—and napping in the early afternoon rather than later in the day. When a nap is too long or too close to bedtime, it can be harder to fall asleep or stay asleep at night.

Another critical component of good sleep hygiene, according to the Mayo Clinic, is to consistently create a restful environment for sleeping. "Keep your bedroom cool, dark and quiet," the organization advises, adding:

> "[Good sleep hygiene consists of] developing helpful, healthy sleep habits and sticking to them."[45]
>
> —Petra Hawker, sleep specialist

47

Exposure to light in the evenings might make it more challenging to fall asleep. Avoid prolonged use of light-emitting screens just before bedtime. Consider using room-darkening shades, earplugs, a fan or other devices to create an environment that suits your needs. Doing calming activities before bedtime, such as taking a bath or using relaxation techniques, might promote better sleep.[46]

Good sleep hygiene also features a short list of substances, activities, and habits to avoid shortly before bed. High on the list, sleep experts emphasize, is staring at computer or cell phone screens, doing heavy exercise, smoking, and consuming caffeine or alcohol. In addition, Matthew Walker states, "avoid large meals and beverages late at night. A light snack is okay, but a large meal can cause indigestion, which interferes with sleep. Drinking too many fluids at night can cause frequent awakenings to urinate. If possible, avoid medicines that delay or disrupt your sleep."[47]

To benefit from napping, experts recommend keeping naps under twenty minutes and napping in the early afternoon rather than later in the day.

Learning from Sleep-Trained Truckers?

Dean Croke, an analyst at DAT Freight & Analytics, a US-based freight company that serves North America, teaches sleep science classes for truckers and other shift workers. He explains that he tries to show them how to obtain better quality sleep with fewer hours in bed. "We build biocompatible schedules," he says, which are "designed around human sleep, as opposed to when the loads must be there." Most people assume that more sleep is better sleep, says Croke, who once worked as a truck driver. But that assumption can be misleading. He goes on, "Our brains sleep in cycles of about an hour and a half." Five ninety-minute sleep cycles would be ideal, he adds, but it is possible to break them up, sleeping two cycles in a row and three cycles later in the day. "I teach drivers to sleep in blocks of an hour and a half. [For truckers] seven hours of sleep is worse than six hours of sleep because seven is not a multiple of an hour and a half."

Quoted in Stephanie Vozza, "What You Can Learn About Sleep from Truckers," *Fast Company*, November 29, 2022. www.fastcompany.com.

Keeping a Sleep Diary

Following all, or even most, of these rules on a regular basis can be difficult at first for the millions of people who are used to practicing poor sleep hygiene. To help oneself ease into better bedtime habits, experts suggest, one can keep a sleep diary. This consists of writing down sleep-related activities each evening for the few days or weeks it takes to get into more healthful habits. Keeping a sleep diary forces a person to look closely at her or his usual routine. This reminds the person which bad habits need fixing the most and helps him or her feel optimistic that those fixes will be successful.

Sleep diaries can take a number of different forms. But according to sleep experts, there are at least some general questions that should be included and that the person keeping the diary should answer each morning when he or she awakens. For example, among the questions recommended by the Sleep Foundation are, "Did you eat a heavy meal or snack after 6:00 p.m.? Did you take any sleeping medication? What medication? What time did you turn off the lights to go to sleep? What time did you wake up? How many total hours did you sleep? How many times did you wake up in the night?"[48]

As the days go by, a person's sleep diary will show, pretty much at a glance, whether she or he is practicing healthy sleep habits. Patterns will inevitably emerge and show the areas in which the person is doing well and those in which improvement is needed. Indeed, Eric Suni of the Sleep Foundation points out, keeping such a diary

> helps people identify sleep disruptions and other factors that can influence sleep quality. Identifying details about habits that affect sleep can show patterns that help explain sleeping problems. . . . Staying current and updating your diary as you go helps avoid any gaps in your memory. For that reason, you want to keep your sleep diary and a pen in an easily accessible place where you'll be reminded to fill it out every day.[49]

Sleeping Pills and Alternative Medicines

Millions of people who have trouble sleeping try to solve the problem by taking sleeping pills of one kind or another. Such sleep aids, nearly all of which are sedatives, are either bought over the counter or prescribed by a doctor.

Although some such pills *will* make a person fall asleep, experts, including many doctors, say that this path to better sleep habits should be avoided in most cases. Rachel Y. Moon explains:

> Sleeping pills are at best a temporary fix. Sedative medications change the quality of sleep, making it less restful, and produce a hangover effect the next day. What's more, if sleep disturbances are the result of habit, sleep medication won't break the cycle. The poor sleeper goes back to his old ways as soon as the medication is stopped. Retraining is required to find ways to sleep better.[50]

Sleeping pills will make a person fall asleep, but experts say that their use should be avoided in most cases. They are a temporary fix and reduce the quality of sleep.

In addition, it is possible for a person to become dependent on a sleeping pill or other ingested sleep aid, no matter whether it is bought over the counter or prescribed by a doctor. And this is especially true in the case of people who have a history of addiction to alcohol, cocaine, or other habit-forming substances. That is why it is vital for a person to tell his or her doctor about any previous or current addiction problems he or she may have. It is also imperative that no one consume a sleep aid along with alcohol, since combining the two can fatally suppress respiration.

Besides sleeping pills and other traditional mainstream sleep aids, a large number of herbal medicines and so-called alternative remedies are routinely marketed as ways to help people get better sleep. A majority of these products claim to have "natural" ingredients. To a great many people, that implies they must be perfectly safe to use because today the term *natural* is often equated with words like *pure* and *healthy*.

The reality, however, is quite frequently very different. "It's important to understand," states a spokesperson for the National

Exercise as a Sleep Aid?

Although there is no doubt that daily exercise improves the quality of sleep, scientists have not discovered why that is the case. "We may never be able to pinpoint the mechanism that explains how [exercise and sleep] are related," says Charlene Gamaldo, medical director of the Johns Hopkins Center for Sleep at Howard County General Hospital in Columbia, Maryland. Nevertheless, she adds, numerous studies have shown that doing moderate aerobic exercise in the course of a day increases the quantity of deep, restful sleep a person gets that night. Also, Gamaldo explains, exercise can help to stabilize mood.

There are differences of opinion as to the best time of day for exercise aimed at improving sleep. Some people claim that exercising close to bedtime causes them to have trouble getting to sleep. In contrast, some others say that the time of day they exercise makes little or no difference. In reality, it probably depends on the person. "Know your body and know yourself," Gamaldo says. "Doctors definitely want you to exercise, but when you do it is not scripted."

Quoted in John Hopkins Medicine, "Exercising for Better Sleep," 2023. www.hopkinsmedicine .org.

Institutes of Health, "that although many herbal or dietary supplements (and some prescription drugs) come from natural sources, 'natural' does not always mean that it's a safer or better option for your health. An herbal supplement may contain dozens of chemical compounds, and all of its ingredients may not be known."[51] It is best, therefore, when considering taking herbal or other sleep aids, to be on the safe side and check with a doctor or pharmacist first.

Sleep experts and most doctors say that one alternative product that can in certain circumstances help people get to sleep is melatonin. A hormone often sold over the counter, it is also produced in small quantities within the human body, mostly during the hours just following sundown. One problem with taking melatonin supplements is that some people naturally make that substance in larger amounts than others do, and for those who do produce larger amounts internally, taking more by mouth may actually hinder rather than induce sleep. Furthermore, science has yet to positively identify the safety of taking melatonin on a long-term basis.

Sleep Clinics and Studies

Using sleeping pills, melatonin, or other oral remedies is often thought of as a last resort among people who do not get enough sleep on a regular basis. They may have first tried to follow the rules of good sleep hygiene, but it did not work for them. They may even have employed sleep diaries, also with negative results. Moreover, if and when they did try taking pills, they ultimately found that they are, as experts point out, a temporary fix at best.

People who feel they have tried everything to get better sleep but to no avail are not members of some small fringe group. Indeed, medical authorities estimate that in the United States alone they make up from 10 to 30 percent of the population. That is somewhere between 33 million and 100 million people.

Whatever their exact numbers may be, members of that army of the sleep deprived can take heart from the good news that there is still hope for them. As the Sleep Foundation's Danielle Pacheco points out, those individuals who have had various difficulties falling or staying asleep over long periods have the hopeful option of visiting a sleep clinic, also called a sleep center. She defines it as "a medical space where sleep testing takes place."

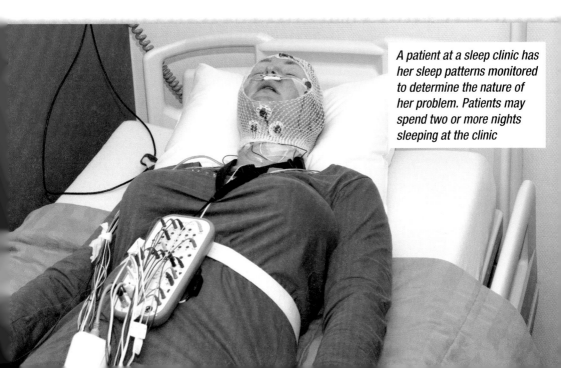

A patient at a sleep clinic has her sleep patterns monitored to determine the nature of her problem. Patients may spend two or more nights sleeping at the clinic

Often, she adds, these highly specialized laboratories also offer "outpatient treatment for people experiencing sleep disorders."[52]

Upon entering such a facility, patients first undergo some basic tests to determine the nature of their problem. In some cases that can include having patients spend two or more nights sleeping in the lab itself, where medical personnel closely monitor them. This step, technically called polysomnography, is most often referred to more simply as a "sleep study." Eventually, the clinic's staff makes a firm diagnosis of the patient's sleep problem and suggests a detailed strategy for overcoming it. After that, a doctor, either the patient's personal physician or one from the clinic, stays in touch and periodically monitors the person's progress in achieving better sleep habits.

The Most Crucial Step

People who undergo a sleep study benefit in two ways. First, they have a better chance of achieving some sort of improvement in their sleeping habits than would otherwise be possible. Second, they become better educated about sleep, its importance, and why people have trouble sleeping. And indeed, sleep experts believe that educating the public about these things will be the single most crucial step in ultimately transforming a sleep-deprived nation into a sleep-satisfied one. "I believe it is time for us to reclaim our right to a full night of sleep," asserts Matthew Walker. "Within the space of a mere hundred years, human beings have abandoned the biologically mandated need for adequate sleep."

> "I believe it is time for us to reclaim our right to a full night of sleep."[53]
>
> —Matthew Walker, sleep scientist and author

But through comprehensively educating all members of society about how to get better sleep, Walker says "we can be reunited with that most powerful elixir of wellness and vitality, dispensed through every conceivable biological pathway. Then we may remember what it feels like to be truly awake during the day, infused with the very deepest plentitude of being."[53]

Source Notes

Introduction: The Biggest Chunk of Human Existence

1. Miguel de Cervantes, *Don Quixote*, trans J.M. Cohen. London: Bohn, 1853, p. 488.
2. Gemma Curtis, "Your Life in Numbers," Dreams, December 8, 2022. www.dreams.co.uk.
3. Centers for Disease Control and Prevention, "Sleep and Sleep Disorders," September 13, 2022. www.cdc.gov.
4. Nicola Sunter, "How Much Sleep Do You Really Need?," Sleepstation, July 19, 2022. www.sleepstation.org.uk.

Chapter One: What Is Sleep, and Why Is It Important?

5. Stuart Wolpert, "UCLA-Led Team of Scientists Discovers Why We Need Sleep," UCLA Newsroom, September 18, 2020. https://newsroom.ucla.edu.
6. Rachel Y. Moon, *Sleep: What Every Parent Needs to Know*. Elk Grove Village, IL: American Academy of Pediatrics, 2013, p. xxiii.
7. Petra Hawker, *Sleep*. New York: DK, 2020, p. 21.
8. Melinda Smith et al., "How Much Sleep Do You Need?," HealthGuide, December 5, 2022. www.helpguide.org.
9. Hawker, *Sleep*, p. 10.
10. Matthew Walker, *Why We Sleep: Unlocking the Power of Sleep and Dreams*. New York: Scribner, 2017, pp. 3–4.
11. Walker, *Why We Sleep*, p. 7.

Chapter Two: Why Is Too Little Sleep So Common?

12. Quoted in Sleepsurge, "84 Famous Sleep Quotes." https://sleepsurge.com.
13. Phil G. Vincent, telephone interview with the author, January 3, 2013.
14. Moon, *Sleep*, p. 131.
15. Nancy Foldvary-Schaefer. *The Cleveland Clinic Guide to Sleep Disorders*. New York: Kaplan, 2009, p. 112.

16. Foldvary-Schaefer, *The Cleveland Clinic Guide to Sleep Disorders*, p. 119.
17. Herbert Ross et al., *Sleep Disorders*. Tiburon, CA: Alternative Medicine, 2000, p. 51.
18. Moon, *Sleep*, p. 24.
19. Hawker, *Sleep*, p. 80.
20. Quoted in Sandee LaMotte, "Sleep Deprivation Affects Nearly Half of American Adults, Study Finds," CNN, November 8, 2022. www.cnn.com.
21. Quoted in LaMotte, "Sleep Deprivation Affects Nearly Half of American Adults, Study Finds."
22. Rob Newsom, "Sleep and Social Media," Sleep Foundation, December 15, 2022. www.sleepfoundation.org.
23. Walker, *Why We Sleep*, p. 269.
24. Sara Martin, "America: A Sleep-Deprived Nation," Wellness Council of America, January 1, 2015. https://shop.welcoa.org.

Chapter Three: Sleep Loss in Young People

25. Heather Turgeon and Julie Wright, *Generation Sleepless*. New York: TarcherPerigee, 2022, pp. 3–4.
26. Walker, *Why We Sleep*, p. 270.
27. Quoted in Sandrine Ceurstemont, "Sleep-Deprived Brains May Be Asleep and Awake at the Same Time," *Horizon*, January 3, 2018. https://ec.europa.eu.
28. Quoted in Kasia Kerridge, "New Colorado Research Shows Pushing Back School Start Times Increases Sleep for Families, Teachers," KKTV, September 7, 2022. www.kktv.com.
29. Eric Suni, "Teens and Sleep," Sleep Foundation, December 15, 2022. www.sleepfoundation.org.
30. Devin Barricklow, "Do I Have Too Many Extracurriculars?," CollegeVine, February 12, 2018. https://blog.collegevine.com.
31. Quoted in Harvard University Summer School, "Why You Should Make a Good Night's Sleep a Priority," May 28, 2021. https://summer.harvard.edu.
32. Moon, *Sleep*, p. 129.
33. Quoted in Harvard University Summer School, "Why You Should Make a Good Night's Sleep a Priority."
34. Eric Suni, "A Study Guide to Getting Sleep During Final Exams," Sleep Foundation, August 29, 2022. www.sleepfoundation.org.

Chapter Four: The Hazards of Getting Too Little Sleep

35. Anjou Khanna Saggi, "How Sleep Deprivation Affects Work-Related Performance," Sleep Cycle, May 5, 2022. www.sleepcycle.com.
36. Gina Wynn, "Sleep Deprivation: An Unseen Hazard in the Workplace," Fisher Scientific, January 15, 2020. www.fishersci.com.
37. Wynn, "Sleep Deprivation."
38. Foundation for Traffic Safety, "Prevalence of Drowsy Driving Crashes: Estimates from a Large-Scale Naturalistic Driving Study," February 1, 2018. https://aaafoundation.org.
39. Talia M. Dunietz, "Drowsy Driving in Teens," Sleep Education, February 5, 2019. https://sleepeducation.org.
40. Georgetta Gregory, "Rail Workers: Deadly Tired but Still Working," *Safety Compass* (blog), National Transportation Safety Board, March 21, 2016. https://safetycompass.wordpress.com.
41. Phyllis C. Zee. "Insomnia and Falls in the Elderly," Medscape, December 28, 2022. www.medscape.org.
42. Quoted in Oxford University Press USA, "Sleep Deprived People More Likely to Have Car Crashes," ScienceDaily, September 18, 2018. www.sciencedaily.com.

Chapter Five: How to Get More and Better Sleep

43. Nick Littlehales, *Sleep*. Boston: Da Capo, 2017, p. 3.
44. Melinda Smith et al., "How to Sleep Better," University of Northwestern St. Paul, August 1, 2015. https://confluence.unwsp.edu.
45. Hawker, *Sleep*, p. 24.
46. Mayo Clinic, "Sleep Tips: 6 Steps to Better Sleep," May 7, 2022. www.mayoclinic.org.
47. Walker, *Why We Sleep*, pp. 341–42.
48. Eric Suni, "Sleep Diary," Sleep Foundation, April 12, 2022. www.sleepfoundation.org.
49. Suni, "Sleep Diary."
50. Moon, *Sleep*, p. 125.
51. National Center for Complementary and Integrative Health, National Institutes of Health, "Natural Doesn't Necessarily Mean Safer, or Better," February 1, 2023. www.nccih.nih.gov.
52. Danielle Pacheco, "Sleep Clinics and Centers," Sleep Foundation, November 8, 2022. www.sleepfoundation.org.
53. Walker, *Why We Sleep*, p. 340.

Organizations and Websites

American Academy of Sleep Medicine (AASM)
https://sleepeducation.org
The AASM website has a sleep education section that includes tabs for information on healthy sleep habits for teens and other age groups, resources for students, informational videos, and tools such as a bedtime calculator.

Centers for Disease Control and Prevention (CDC)
www.cdc.gov
The CDC's main mission is to protect the health of the American people by detecting and investigating health problems, including a chronic lack of sleep. A hefty section of the website tells young people how they can get internships in which to study health problems such as sleep deprivation.

Sleep Foundation
www.sleepfoundation.org
The mission of the Sleep Foundation (formerly the National Sleep Foundation) is to alert the public, health care providers, and public policy makers to the life-and-death importance of adequate sleep. Its helpful website contains dozens of links to sleep-related topics, including one relating to the sleep needs of teens and other young people.

Why Sleep Is Important, American Psychological Association
www.apa.org/topics/sleep/why.aspx?item=1
One of the most respected medical organizations in the world offers this collection of links to mini-articles about sleep and its importance for good health, including emotional and mental health.

For Further Research

Books

Barbara Herkert and Daniel Long, *Sleep*. Park Ridge, IL: Albert Whitman, 2022.

William F. Hill, *Get Instant Healthy Sleep Cycle*. Self-published, Amazon Digital Services, 2022. Kindle.

Leanne Kabat and Angela Kim, *Teens Talk About Mental Health*. Kabat Media, 2022.

Lisa L. Lewis, *The Sleep Deprived Teen*. Miami, FL: Margo, 2022.

Matthew Walker, *Why We Sleep*. New York: Scribner, 2018.

Internet Sources

Anita Busch, "Hollywood's Grueling Hours & Drowsy-Driving Problem: Crew Members Speak Out Despite Threat to Careers," Deadline, February 1, 2018. https://deadline.com.

Sandrine Ceurstemont, "Sleep-Deprived Brains May Be Asleep and Awake at the Same Time," *Horizon*, January 3, 2018. https://ec.europa.eu.

Gemma Curtis, "Your Life in Numbers," Dreams, December 8, 2022. www.dreams.co.uk.

Gallup, "Casper-Gallup State of Sleep in America 2022 Report," June 1, 2022. www.gallup.com.

Juliann Garey, "Why Are Teens So Sleep Deprived?," Child Mind Institute, October 12, 2021. https://childmind.org.

Sandee LaMotte, "Sleep Deprivation Affects Nearly Half of American Adults, Study Finds," CNN, November 8, 2022. www.cnn.com.

Mayo Clinic, "Sleep Tips: 6 Steps to Better Sleep," May 7, 2022. www.mayoclinic.org.

Danielle Pacheco, "Drowsy Driving vs. Drunk Driving: How Similar Are They?," Sleep Foundation, June 24, 2022. www.sleepfoundation.org.

Danielle Pacheco, "Sleep Clinics and Centers," Sleep Foundation, November 8, 2022. www.sleepfoundation.org.

Arianna Sarjoo, "Nearly 3 in 10 Americans Have Insomnia: Survey," WebMD, June 4, 2022. www.webmd.com.

Eric Suni, "Sleep Hygiene," Sleep Foundation, September 29, 2022. www.sleepfoundation.org.

Eric Suni, "Sleep Statistics," Sleep Foundation, May 13, 2022. www.sleepfoundation.org.

Stephani Vozza, "What You Can Learn About Sleep from Truckers," *Fast Company*, November 29, 2022. www.fastcompany.com.

Stuart Wolpert, "UCLA-Led Team of Scientists Discovers Why We Need Sleep," UCLA Newsroom, September 18, 2020. https://newsroom.ucla.edu.

Index

Picture Credits